CHILDREN'S BRITANNICA

HISTORY QUIZ

Devised by
the Editors of
CHILDREN'S BRITANNICA

ON

G[illegible]ada Publishing

Dragon Books
Granada Publishing Ltd
8 Grafton Street, London W1X 3LA

Published by Dragon Books 1984

A Dragon Original

Encyclopaedia Britannica International, Limited
Mappin House, 156–162 Oxford Street, London W1N 0HJ

British Library Cataloguing in Publication Data
Children's Britannica history quiz –
(Children's Britannica quiz book series; 3)
1. World history – Juvenile literature
909 D21

ISBN 0-583-30661-6

Reproduced, printed and bound in Great Britain by
Hazell Watson & Viney Limited,
Aylesbury, Bucks

Set in Century Schoolbook

CHILDREN'S BRITANNICA

HISTORY QUIZ

CONTENTS

ABOUT THIS QUIZ BOOK

The word 'history' comes from *historia*, a Greek word meaning 'knowledge obtained by inquiry'. In other words, history is what we learn by asking questions. What better subject, then, for a quiz book – which is full of questions?

In this book you will find quizzes on all kinds of topics and questions on all kinds of subjects . . . famous people, inventions, great events from the past, recent history, science, sport. You don't have to be a history expert, of course. Some questions are more difficult than others, but as you go through the book you'll find that you're improving your general knowledge as well as being baffled occasionally!

For example, did you know that the Teddy Bear got its name from a President of the United States . . . that cave people lived on top of a rubbish heap . . . or that the humble mole was once honoured by a king's enemies? You'll find the answers to all the questions at the back of the book. (They begin on page 84.) But try answering the questions first, without looking at the answers! You can do each quiz on your own, just for fun, or you can run your own quiz contest at home. With this book in your hands, you can be a quiz superstar.

Two Centuries of History

History can cover almost anything . . . the history of music, for example, or painting, or aviation, and so on. Encyclopaedias contain an awful lot of history. And some have become part of history themselves.

Encyclopaedia Britannica is probably the most famous English-language encyclopaedia. It began in 1768 during the reign of George III (1760 to 1820) and is still around seven reigns later. (Can you name the seven British monarchs since George III? Answers at the foot of the page.)

That period of history has seen many important events. In fact, in the past 200 years the whole world has changed, almost beyond recognition. When *Encyclopaedia Britannica* was first published in 1768, oxygen had not been discovered (1774), the United States had not declared its independence (1776) and no-one had flown in a balloon (1783). 'High technology' in those days was the newly invented steam engine. In fact, James Watt, the pioneer of steam power, was one of the experts who wrote articles for the early editions of *Encyclopaedia Britannica.*

Answers to 'seven monarchs' teaser.

George IV (1820–30), William IV (1830–37), Victoria (1837–1901), Edward VII (1901–10), George V (1910–36), George VI (1936–52), Elizabeth II (1952–)

STONE AGE QUIZ

Did You Know . . . that the mammoth was hunted by early man? These large, woolly elephants died out about 10,000 years ago. Whole mammoths have been dug up from the frozen soil of Siberia (USSR).

1 Was *Australopithecus* . . .
  a) an early type of human?
  b) an extinct reptile?
  c) a fossil Australian fruit?

2 Which did early man learn first: how to hunt or how to grow crops?

3 Trace the dots to find out what animal this Stone Age artist drew on the cave wall.

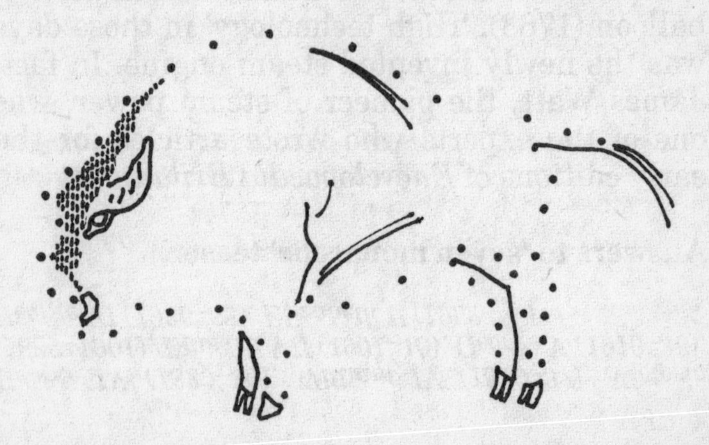

LIVING ON A RUBBISH HEAP

Did you know that the prehistoric cave dwellers lived, quite literally, on top of a rubbish heap? Inside their caves, they never cleared away the ashes of their fires nor did they bother to throw out the bones of the animals they ate. If a person died, the dead body was usually buried in a shallow hole in the floor.

Generations of people lived in the same caves. So the pile of rubbish inside went on growing until it formed a layer of what scientists call 'cave-earth'. Today, this rubbish is a treasure-trove of information about prehistoric people. It tells us not only what they ate but also (since tool-makers never bothered to clear up their flint chippings) what kind of stone tools they used. In fact, rubbish tips are 'time capsules' of information for archaeologists.

So the next time you throw something away, remember that in a few hundred years it could well be a valuable archaeological 'find'!

ANCIENT EGYPT

1 These are the three most famous pyramids, built by the kings of Egypt over 4,500 years ago. The largest is that of King Cheops or Khufu. How many stone blocks do you think were used to build it?

a) 250,000   b) 1 million   c) 2.3 million

2 Here are three Egyptian gods, all wrongly named. Can you give their correct names?

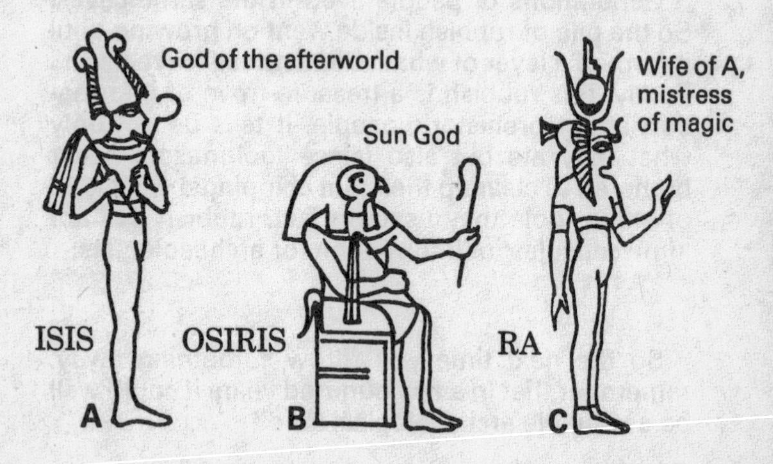

3 These are 'hieroglyphs' – the picture-signs the Egyptians used for writing. An Egyptian clerk might also have needed 'papyrus'. What for?

4 Who was this boy-king of ancient Egypt? His tomb was found in 1922, in the Valley of the Kings. This gold face mask had been placed on the boy-king's mummy.

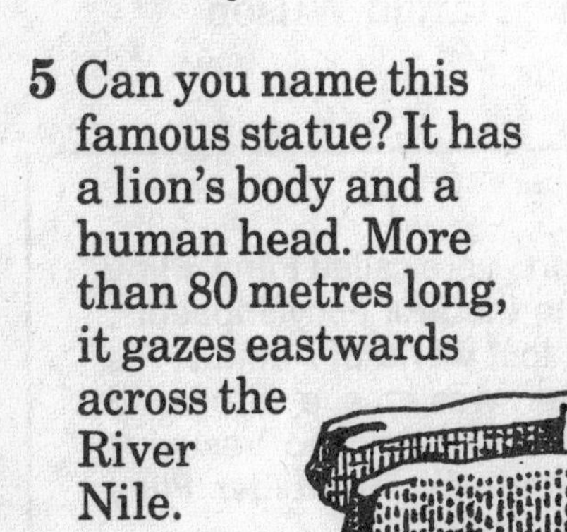

5 Can you name this famous statue? It has a lion's body and a human head. More than 80 metres long, it gazes eastwards across the River Nile.

THE NAME'S THE SAME

Sometimes it can be confusing when several famous people share the same surname. Can you spot the person described in the clue?

1 A President of the United States
Gerald Ford   Henry Ford   John Ford

2 A 19th-century traveller in West Africa
Henry Kingsley   Charles Kingsley
Mary Kingsley

3 A desert soldier
E. O. Lawrence   D. H. Lawrence
T. E. Lawrence

4 A pioneer aviator
Lyndon Johnson   Amy Johnson
Jack Johnson

5 A British prime minister
Woodrow Wilson   Harold Wilson
Angus Wilson

Two Famous Plinys

Two famous Roman writers were called Pliny. Pliny the Elder (AD 23–79) wrote the first encyclopaedia, and also wrote about the lost world of Atlantis. His nephew, Pliny the Younger, was an eye-witness to the disaster in AD 79 when the volcano Vesuvius destroyed the town of Pompeii. The elder Pliny died during the terrible eruption.

THE ROOSEVELTS

Two US Presidents shared the name Roosevelt. Theodore ('Teddy') was born in 1858 and was President from 1901 to 1909. He loved the outdoor life, and gave his name to the 'Teddy Bear'. He died in 1919.

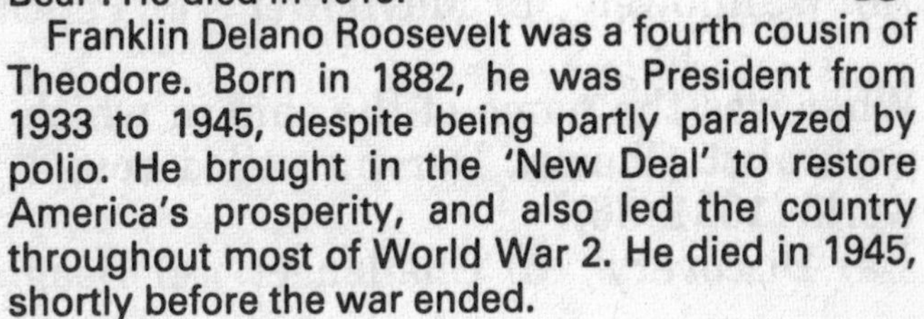

Franklin Delano Roosevelt was a fourth cousin of Theodore. Born in 1882, he was President from 1933 to 1945, despite being partly paralyzed by polio. He brought in the 'New Deal' to restore America's prosperity, and also led the country throughout most of World War 2. He died in 1945, shortly before the war ended.

6 He was rescued by an Indian girl called Pocahontas

Adam Smith John Smith
Sydney Smith

7 The first Englishman to visit Japan, in 1600

William Adams Walter Adams
John Adams

8 A scientist who studied the atom

Mark Rutherford Margaret Rutherford
Ernest Rutherford

And Two Famous Pitts

Two British prime ministers have been Pitts. William Pitt the Elder led Britain during the Seven Years' War (1756–63). His second son, William Pitt the Younger, became prime minister in 1783 at the age of only 24. He was the country's leader during the early part of the Napoleonic Wars and introduced income tax (to help pay for the war).

FAMOUS SHIPS

1 In 1620 the Pilgrim Fathers set sail from Plymouth to make a new home in America. What was the name of their ship?
a) 'Wallflower' b) 'Mayflower' c) 'Pelican'

2 What was the name of the ship in which the naturalist Charles Darwin sailed round the world (1831–36)?
a) 'Discovery' b) 'Challenger' c) 'Beagle'

3 What made HMS 'Warrior' of 1860 ahead of its time?
a) it was the first steamship
b) it was the first all-iron armoured ship
c) it was the first screw-driven ship

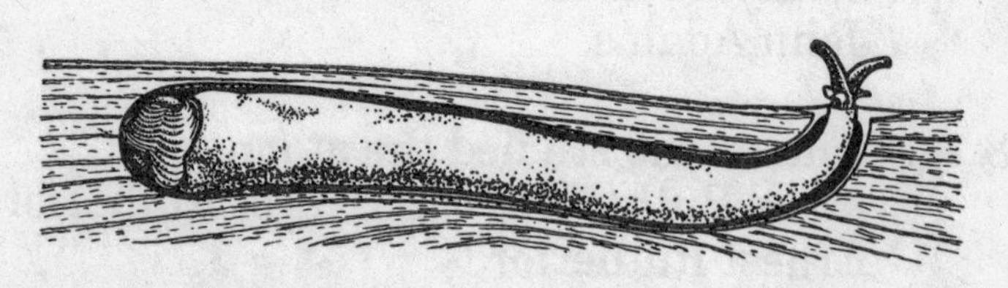

DID YOU KNOW . . .

. . . that wooden ships were riddled with worms? The teredo or shipworm is a sea mollusc which bores holes in timber, soon reducing a wooden hull to a fragile honeycomb. Wooden ships were very vulnerable to shipworm attack until in the 18th century shipbuilders began to plate the bottoms of vessels with copper sheathing.

4 What was the name of Admiral Nelson's flagship at the battle of Trafalgar?

5 Who commanded the US warship 'Bon Homme Richard' against the British 'Serapis' in 1779?

6 A German battleship was scuttled after a fight with British cruisers at the Battle of the River Plate in 1939. Was its name . . .
a) 'Tirpitz' b) 'Bismarck' c) 'Graf Spee'

7 Which ocean liner was the last holder of the Blue Riband for fastest crossing of the Atlantic?
a) 'Queen Mary' b) 'United States'
c) 'France'

8 What is the name of the Tudor warship recovered from the sea bed of the English Channel in 1982?
a) 'Great Harry b) 'White Ship'
c) 'Mary Rose'

9 Was the USS 'Nautilus' (1954) . . .
a) the world's first nuclear submarine?
b) the last battleship to be launched?
c) the holder of the deep-diving record?

10 See if you can match these famous ships with their famous commanders.

'Revenge'	Christopher Columbus
'Golden Hind'	James Cook
'Endeavour'	Sir Richard Grenville
'Santa Maria'	Sir Francis Drake

WILD WEST

1 Which famous US marshal brought law and order to Dodge City, Kansas and Tombstone, Arizona? He took part in a famous gunfight at the OK Corral.

2 By what nicknames were these three better known?
   a) William Bonney   b) William F. Cody
   c) Martha Canary (alias Martha Burke)

3 What was a 'prairie schooner'?

4 In 1869 at Promontory, Utah a 'Golden Spike' was driven to mark an historic event. What?

5 Most cowboys carried a lariat. Was this a whip, a knife, or a lasso?

6 In 1876 the Sioux Indians, led by Chief Sitting Bull, won the battle of the Little Bighorn River. Who lost the battle?

7 What were *chaparajos*, or chaps?

8 Of which Indian people was Geronimo a leader?
   a) Cheyenne   b) Apache   c) Navaho

9 Which famous frontiersman was born in Tennessee in 1786 and died at the Alamo, Texas in 1836?

THE PONY EXPRESS

From St Joseph, Missouri to Sacramento, California (some 2,900 kilometres) in just 10 days! That was the boast of the Pony Express. Sea mail took a month. Stagecoaches could do no better than 25 days. This was in 1860, when the western settlers clamoured for better links with the eastern United States. So the Pony Express bought 500 fast horses and set up 190 relay stations. And the race was on.

Each rider was tough and hard-riding, but preferably lightweight. Carrying the mail in a leather pouch, he galloped his mount until it was exhausted (about 25 km at most), then leaped on to a fresh horse. Defying hostile Indians, bad weather and rough country, the Pony Express lost only one shipment of mail.

Yet, in October 1861, just 18 months after it began, the Pony Express went out of business. What had beaten it? The new telegraph wires crossing the American continent!

FACT OR FICTION?

History and make-believe often get mixed up so that it is hard to tell fact from fiction. Were these people real-life characters or do they only exist in stories? (Tick the boxes.)

	Fact	Fiction
1 Robin Hood		
2 Dick Turpin		
3 Buffalo Bill		
4 Captain Bligh		
5 Lancelot of the Lake		
6 El Cid		
7 The Man in the Iron Mask		
8 Rob Roy		
9 Kit Carson		
10 Sherlock Holmes		
11 Alexander the Great		
12 The Scarlet Pimpernel		

El Dorado – Just a Dream?

In the 1500s Spanish adventurers sailed across the Atlantic to South America. They hoped to find *El Dorado*, or 'the gilded one'. This is what the first Spanish explorers called the chief of an Indian tribe who was supposed to cover himself with gold dust as part of a religious ceremony. Excited by such tales, the Spanish hunted for El Dorado, and in time the name was given to an imaginary kingdom, full of treasure.

The Spanish conquerors did indeed find much gold in the New World. But they never found El Dorado – although some claimed to have seen the 'golden man' himself. Today, the expression El Dorado is used to mean a dream country, forever out of reach.

Incredible Birds

The Roc was a fabulous bird, according to *The Arabian Nights*. It was of enormous size, large enough to carry off elephants to feed its young! It could easily fly off with a man (such as the adventurous Sindbad the Sailor).

Of course, the Roc is only a storybook creation, not a real bird at all.

But, giant birds *did* live, and not long ago. On the island of Madagascar lived the Elephant Bird, 3 metres tall and weighing 500 kg. Neither it nor the Moa of New Zealand (half as heavy but taller) could fly. Both died out between 1700 and 1850, hunted by man.

WHEN IN ROME . . .

1 Who were the twin brothers who, according to legend, founded the city of ancient Rome?

2 Beside which river was Rome built?

3 The *Curia* was an important building in Rome: was it a) a market for antiques, b) the meeting-place of the government or c) the public swimming pool?

4 What was the language of the people of Rome?

Picture Question. Fill in the missing letters. This ancient Roman is a P—————————, one of the rich and powerful people of the city. He is wearing a T———. If he were a S———————, a member of the government, his garment would have a border coloured P————— to show his rank.

5 What sort of birds were kept as 'watch dogs' by the Romans to warn them of surprise attacks?

6 True or false . . .?
- **a** Roman homes had no windows, because the Romans could not make glass.
- **b** The Romans disapproved of doctors, and kept slaves trained in medicine to look after their families.
- **c** Most important of the gods which they worshipped was Pluto, king of the gods.

7 The people who belonged to the poorer classes were called P---------. Fill in the letters.

8 The ruins of this huge stadium, where gladiators once fought, can still be seen in Rome. What is its name?

MAGIC MILK

The Romans loved make-up and beauty rituals. One recipe for whitening the face contained, among other things, 'barley of Libya, lentils, peeled narcissus bulbs and gum arabic'. Baths were particularly popular. The men bathed in wine, while the women believed that in a bath of asses' milk 'lurked a magic which would dispel all diseases and blights from beauty'.

FAMOUS BATTLES

What decides who wins a battle? Throughout history military experts have puzzled over this question. It's tempting to say 'The side with the biggest army wins', but that has not always been so. It has been said that four principles, or rules, can affect a battle.

a) Concentration
b) Surprise
c) Co-operation
d) Mobility

And we can add a fifth: e) Luck!

Take a look at the pictures, and see if you can guess which of these five principles each picture illustrates. It's easy really!

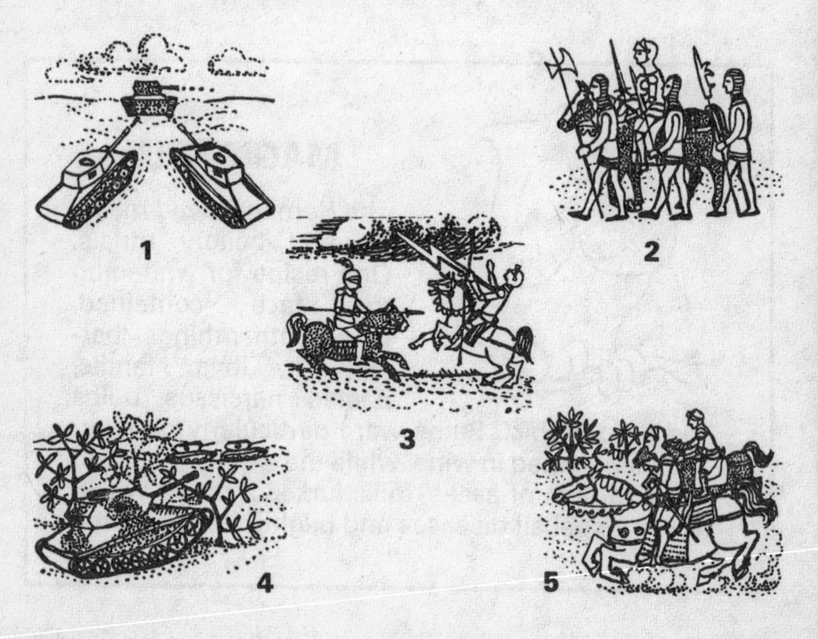

Can you identify these famous battles?
Clue: See names in box below.

1 This battle was fought between the Ancient Greeks and the Persians. After the Greeks won, a famous runner called Pheidippides ran about 24 miles to carry the news to Athens.

2 Henry V of England won this battle, in 1415, defeating the French.

3 This sea battle of 1905 was the first big naval battle fought with guns and torpedoes by armoured battleships. The Japanese fleet defeated the Russians.

4 During this battle, the English king was slain by an arrow in the eye, and the Norman invaders won.

5 After this battle, in 1781, the American War of Independence quickly came to an end.

6 The opposing commanders in this desert battle, fought in 1942, were the German general Rommel and the British general Montgomery.

ALAMEIN HASTINGS YORKTOWN MARATHON TSHUSHIMA AGINCOURT

REFORMERS

1 This American president wanted to stop the spread of slavery and led the victorious North in the American Civil War. His name was A——— L———.

2 a) In London's Piccadilly Circus stands this famous statue. What is its name?

b) The statue was put up in memory of Anthony Ashley Cooper, 7th Earl of S————————. He helped to pass laws stopping women and children from working in coal mines. He also helped to improve housing and schools.

3 What was the Diet of Worms?

Was it
a) a time of famine and hardship during the French Revolution?
b) a revolt by German peasants during the Middle Ages?
c) a council called to question the Protestant leader Martin Luther?

4 Who is this? She . . .
. . . worked at Scutari in the Crimea
. . . is called the 'founder of modern nursing'
. . . was known as 'the lady with the lamp'

5 Is the name of William Wilberforce known for
   a) prison reform?
   b) helping to abolish slavery?
   c) working for better health conditions?

6 a) Pennsylvania is a state of the USA named after its founder. What was his name?
   b) The colony was founded as a place where all its people could live in peace. They wanted to share in its government and be free from religious persecution. The name of Pennsylvania's capital means 'brotherly love'. Is it . . .
      a) Delaware?
      b) Delphi?
      c) Philadelphia?

7 Can you arrange these letters into a famous political slogan?

ESTOV ROF MENWO

This slogan was heard in London in the cause of the suffragettes. Who was their leader?

A True School Story

The story *Tom Brown's Schooldays* tells of life at Rugby School in England during the early 19th century. In those days, boarding schools were rough places where bullying, gambling and drinking took place. A new headmaster changed Rugby completely, raising the standard of work, finding masters that the pupils could admire, and encouraging sport. His name was Dr Thomas Arnold and his ideas on education soon spread to many other schools. *Tom Brown's Schooldays* was written by one of his pupils, Thomas Hughes.

EUREKA!

1 In 1543 this Polish astronomer declared that the Earth turns once every 24 hours and that it moves round the Sun. His name?
C––––––––s

2 Francis Bacon was a famous 16th-century scientist. One snowy day while out in his carriage, he stopped to buy a fowl, which he then stuffed with snow. Sadly, he also caught a chill which caused his death. What was Francis Bacon trying to find out through this strange experiment?

3 Who discovered what? Fill in the correct name to link the scientist with his discovery.

FLEMING JENNER PRIESTLEY

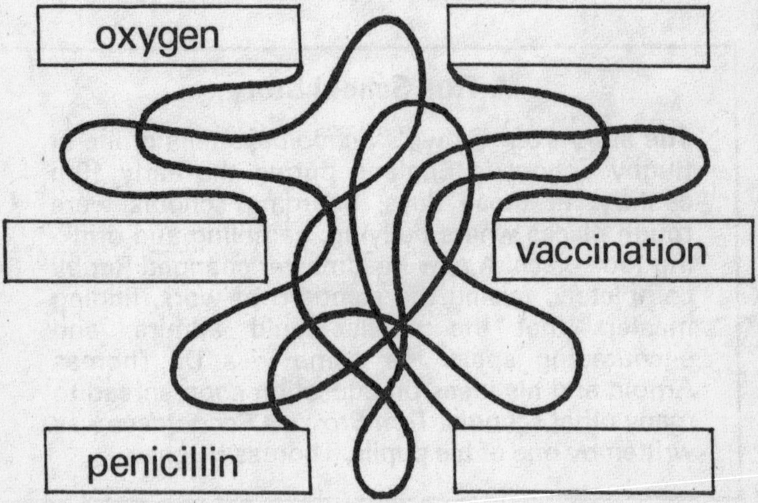

oxygen

vaccination

penicillin

4 How many inventions did Thomas Alva Edison patent . . . 20, 50, 100, 1000? And, can you name his best known invention, used in almost every home when it gets dark?

5 Pair the scientist with the invention or discovery.

Newton	antiseptics
Einstein	X-rays
Trevithick	calculating machine
Lister	gravity
Pascal	steam locomotive
Marconi	relativity
Roentgen	radio telegraphy

6 Benjamin Franklin helped to draw up the American Declaration of Independence. He also went kite-flying in a thunderstorm. What invention did this lead to?

ARCHIMEDES

The word *Eureka* is associated with this story about Archimedes, the Greek inventor. A king wanted to know if his crown was made of pure gold. It was a puzzle that Archimedes couldn't solve. Then one day at bathtime he noticed how the water in the bath rose when he stepped in. Suddenly he knew how to solve the problem. He ran naked into the street shouting *Eureka* ('I've found it'). He took the crown and a piece of pure gold of the same weight. Then he put them one at a time into a vessel of water. The amount of liquid which over-flowed each time was different. This showed that the crown was not pure gold.

PRIME MINISTERS

How much do you know about British prime ministers?

1 Which of these was *not* prime minister?
William Pitt Charles James Fox
Henry Addington

2 Which British prime minister was a famous general and nicknamed the 'Iron Duke'?

3 Which prime minister introduced income tax?

4 Which prime minister borrowed £4 million to buy shares in the Suez Canal?

5 Who was the youngest prime minister of the 20th century?

6 Who was the first Labour prime minister?
a) Lloyd George b) Ramsay MacDonald
c) Clement Attlee

7 Which prime minister had the Christian names William Ewart?

8 In what year did Margaret Thatcher become prime minister?

9 Which prime minister founded the London police force in 1829?

10 Who was the prime minister in 1939, when World War 2 began?
a) Neville Chamberlain
b) Winston Churchill c) Stanley Baldwin

The last two questions are about prime ministers of other countries.

11 Which country had the first woman prime minister?
a) India b) Sri Lanka c) Canada

12 Of which countries were these people the prime ministers?

Eamon De Valera	Canada
Robert Menzies	France
Lester Pearson	Ireland
Georges Pompidou	New Zealand
Keith Holyoake	Australia

The First 'First Minister'

Sir Robert Walpole (1676–1745) is generally thought of as Britain's first Prime Minister. Until 1717 the King or Queen had led the meetings of the 'Cabinet' of chief ministers. George I, however, spoke no English, and stopped going to Cabinet meetings. From 1721 Walpole led its discussions, so becoming Prime ('First') Minister. For a long time, though, no-one liked the idea and the title 'Prime Minister' came into use only slowly.

WHO WAS . . . ?

Clues: See box on page 29.

1 The leader of the Peasants' Revolt of 1381 in England

2 The American showman who boasted he had 'the greatest show on earth' in the three-ring circus he owned (with his partner Bailey)

3 The Austrian doctor who developed psycho-analysis – the examination of the mind

4 The Polish scientist who discovered radium and won two Nobel prizes

5 The US President who was a leading General during the American Civil War

6 The wife of King Louis XVI of France, who was beheaded in 1793

7 The leader of the Mormon migration to the Great Salt Lake in Utah, USA in 1847

8 The English general who captured Quebec from the French in 1759

9 The navigator who was the first to sail round Australia, and also discovered New Zealand

10 The German statesman who was known as the 'Iron Chancellor'

11 The first woman aviator to fly solo across the Atlantic Ocean, in 1932

12 The country doctor who discovered a method of fighting the disease smallpox, by inoculation

Marie Curie	Otto von Bismarck
James Wolfe	Sigmund Freud
Edward Jenner	Ulysses S. Grant
P. T. Barnum	Amelia Earhart
Wat Tyler	Abel Tasman
Brigham Young	Marie Antoinette

MYSTERY MAN

Can you guess the name of our mystery man? Here are some clues to help you.

He was born in 1720.

His grandfather was a king who lost his throne.

His father tried, but failed, to regain that throne.

He was born and died in exile, in Rome, far from the land he hoped to rule.

In 1745 he led a revolt, hoping to become a king himself. But it failed, and he had to flee, disguised as a maidservant.

INITIALS QUIZ

Choose the right set of initials to answer each clue. Then write out the words in full, making sure that they fit the spaces provided.

E.E.C.	S.E.A.T.O.	F.B.I.
G.B.	U.K.	U.S.S.R.
N.A.T.O.	U.N.	W.H.O.
O.A.U.	U.N.E.S.C.O.	
S.A.L.T.	U.N.I.C.E.F.	

1 One of the 'super powers'.

_____ __ ______ _________
____

2 Successor to the League of Nations.

______ _______

3 Established by the Treaty of Rome (1957).

________ ________ _________

4 All its member countries are African.

____________ __ _______ _____

5 This American organization is famous for tracking down gangsters and spies.

_______ ______ __ _____________

6 No country in the South Atlantic could be a member of this.

_____ ________ ______

____

7 An island off the coast of Europe.

_____ _______

8 A healthy part of **2**.

_____ ______ ____________

9 Set up in 1954, its members included New Zealand, Thailand and the Philippines.

_________ ____ ______

____

10 Sounds bitter, but in fact it was an agreement on disarmament, signed between the United States and the Soviet Union.

_________ ____ __________ ______

11 Emergency help for the world's children.

______ _______ _____________

_________ _________ ____

12 Bigger than **7**, but smaller than the British Isles.

______ ________

13 Another part of **2**: this organization is not just educational.

______ _______ ___________

__________ ___ ________

____

WARRIORS

1 This famous Greek warrior was killed by an arrow wound in his heel, the only part of his body not protected by magic. Who was he?
ACHILLES   AGAMEMNON   ULYSSES

2 The Swiss were famous for their skill with the 'halberd'. What kind of weapon was this?
a) an early gunpowder musket
b) a long spear with an axe head
c) a broad sword with jagged edges

3 In which ancient army were there *centurions* and *cohorts*?

4 *Picture Question.* Can you date the armour shown below?

Clues: Greek   Norman   Roman   13th century

5 The *samurai* were proud warriors who would kill themselves rather than surrender. In which country did the samurai live?

THE WARRIOR CODE

The Vikings believed that warriors killed in battle went to Valhalla to feast with the gods. The Anglo-Saxons too had a strong belief in the warrior code. A man was expected to fight for his lord, and warriors who fought bravely were praised as heroes.

One of the oldest English poems tells of the heroism of the Anglo-Saxons at the battle of Maldon (Essex) in the year 991. The enemy was familiar, the invading Northmen. The defenders fought bravely, but their leader was killed, and the battle was lost. What mattered most, according to the poet, was the loyalty and courage of the warriors in fighting and dying for their lord. In this way, a small, unimportant battle became celebrated in one of the greatest poems left to us by the Anglo-Saxons.

WHAT DID THEY WEAR?

The clothes people wear have changed a lot over the years. Here are a few wardrobe items from past centuries. Can you identify each one correctly? *Clues*: See box.

1 A loose cloth garment worn by Romans

2 A short, padded coat worn by men in the Middle Ages

3 A wire 'cage', worn by women in Victorian times to keep their skirts full

4 Loose-fitting breeches, gathered in at the knee, popular in the 1870s

5 A laced tunic worn by women in the Middle Ages

DOUBLET KNICKERBOCKERS TOGA
CRINOLINE KIRTLE

The Devil's Own Dress!

In the 1300s courtiers wore long tight hose, or stockings, to show off their legs – sometimes each stocking being a different colour. A serious-minded monk complained that they looked more like devils than men!

Picture Puzzle. Look at the pictures, then date each style of dress, from the descriptions given below.

About 1905	1800 to 1820
Ancient Greek	About 1840
Puritans 1640	1920s
Ancient Egyptians	Early 1200s

PRESIDENTIAL PUZZLERS

These questions are all about presidents of the United States.

1 The first president of the United States gave his name to the nation's capital. Who was he? W---------

2 The third president was, before his election, the main writer of the Declaration of Independence. J--------

3 This president took office in 1861, the year the American Civil War broke out. What was his name? L------

4 He had to resign as president following the 'Watergate' scandal. Who was he? N----

5 This president campaigned to set up the League of Nations after the end of World War 1. W-----

6 He became president just weeks before the end of World War 2. Who was he? T-----

7 This president, who served for two terms during the 1950s, had the nickname 'Ike'. What was his real name? E---------

FACT FILE

The longest-serving president was Franklin Roosevelt, elected four times.

Four presidents have been assassinated in office: Lincoln, Garfield, McKinley and Kennedy

Only one president, Andrew Johnson, has been put on trial by his government. Verdict: not guilty.

8 Elected in 1960, he was the youngest man ever to become president. K-------

9 His business was peanut farming before he won the 1976 election. C------

Puzzle. Can you spot the names of seven U.S. presidents hidden in the word square?

X	R	T	W	O	T	B
T	E	E	N	Q	U	I
F	A	K	V	A	N	R
A	G	J	Y	O	R	F
T	A	A	X	U	O	G
G	N	I	D	R	A	H
Z	N	A	D	A	M	S

WHO SAID . . . ?

1 Take one word from each line to find the answer Queen Marie-Antoinette is supposed to have given when told that the poor people of France had no bread.

See Smell Let Find Hit
us we you all them
drink eat swallow sneeze
orange tea cake water

2 A famous automobile maker said *History is bunk*.
Was it . . . Gottlieb Daimler? Charles Rolls? Henry Ford? Henry Royce?

3 After a victory in Asia, Julius Caesar said, 'I came, I saw, I conquered'. But, of course, he said it in Latin. What is the right order for his three words?

Vidi Vici Veni *Vici Veni Vidi*
Veni Vidi Vici

4 Who said in a Shakespeare play, *A horse! a horse! My kingdom for a horse*?

The Man in a Barrel

Diogenes was a philosopher of ancient Greece who died about 320 BC. He wanted to own nothing, and is said to have lived in a tub. A story is told of him that he walked about carrying a lighted lantern during the daytime. When asked why, he said 'I am searching for an honest man'. He is also famous for the reply he gave to Alexander the Great, who visited him. When Alexander asked if Diogenes wanted anything, he answered, 'Stand a little less between me and the Sun'.

---

5 A *England is a nation of shopkeepers*
B *Let not poor Nelly starve*
C *Dr Livingstone, I presume*
D *I am the state*
E *Who will rid me of this turbulent priest?*
F *You cannot fool all the people all the time*
G *Patriotism is not enough*

Above are some famous quotations. Below are the names of the people who said them. Choose the right name to fit the quotation.
Henry II   Abraham Lincoln   Napoleon
Edith Cavell   Louis XIV
H. M. Stanley   Charles II

6 Who is supposed to have said *We are not amused*?

7 When asked who had chopped down his father's cherry tree, this truthful boy replied, 'Father, I cannot tell a lie, I did it with my little hatchet'. The boy grew up to become an important American. Who was he?

FAMOUS DATES

1 1666 .... Why were Londoners carrying buckets of water and making for boats on the Thames?

2 1815 .... What was Copenhagen doing so close to Brussels?

3 43 AD .... What had they seen coming towards them that made the ancient Britons turn blue?

4 1492 .... Who went sailing in three ships across the ocean blue?

5 1849 .... What made so many people rush to sunny California?

6 1588 .... Why were beacons set blazing on English hillsides?

7 1066 .... What happened to make the ladies of Bayeux get busy with their needles?

8 September 27, 1825 .... People had bought tickets to be taken for a ride. Why was this so special?

9 1917 .... In which country did millions of people decide that they should become comrades?

10 1847 .... What made thousands of starving Irish people leave home for the USA?

11 July 20, 1969 .... Where had the Eagle arrived when it landed in the Sea of Tranquillity?

The Wrong Months

Septem, octo, novem and decem are the Latin words for 7, 8, 9 and 10. We use them in the names of our months September, October, November and December. That seems simple. But . . . September is the 9th month of the year, not the 7th. Why? Well, to begin with, the Romans had a calendar with only ten months in a year. It started in March, so that September was the 7th month. Around 700 BC they added an extra two months – January and February – and all the other months were pushed back. September now became the 9th month of the year as we know it today.

ASSASSINATIONS

1 Who was this man? He was
. . . a famous Indian leader greatly admired
. . . killed in 1948 by a religious fanatic
. . .called 'Mahatma', meaning 'Great Soul'

2 This famous family lived in Italy at the time of the Renaissance. They . . .
. . . came originally from Spain
. . . had two popes in the family – Calixtus III and Alexander VI
. . . were ruthless in killing their enemies, and often used poison.
They were called the B------s.

3 Can you fill in the missing name on this family tree? It belongs to a king of England who is famous as a wicked uncle.

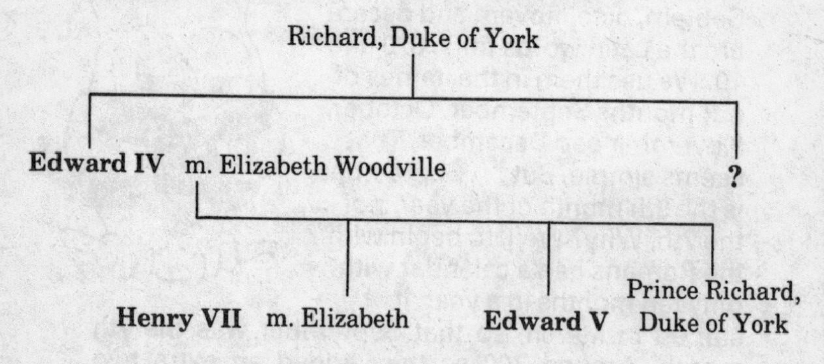

4 Who was the famous Roman leader killed . . .
. . . at the Senate House in Rome
. . . on the Ides of March in 44 BC

5 a Fill in the gaps.
John Wilkes Booth shot Abraham Lincoln at the t------e in Washington, DC, USA. Lee Harvey Oswald shot John Kennedy in D------, Texas, USA.

b The two victims were both – what?

The 'Old Man of the Mountain'

The 'assassins' belonged to a secret religious sect which grew up in Iran in the Middle ages. Their chief was called the 'Old Man of the Mountain' by Crusaders from Europe. As their religious duty, his followers had to kill enemies of the sect, and for 200 years they held the area in terror. Before setting out on their deadly task, they took the drug 'hashish'. From 'hashish' comes the word 'assassin'.

6 In 1567 a house in Edinburgh, Scotland, was blown up. The queen's husband, Lord Darnley, was killed. Some people said that the queen knew he was to be murdered. Who was the queen?

7 The assassination of the Austrian Archduke Francis Ferdinand led to a war. Which war?
a) The Franco-Prussian War
b) The Boer War
c) World War 1
d) The war of the Austrian Succession

8 In 1940 in Mexico a famous Russian revolutionary leader was murdered. Was he . . .
a) Stalin? b) Lenin? c) Trotsky?

MONUMENTS

A monument is a memorial – a building, a statue, an arch – to mark some great event in history. Can you identify the six shown here, and say what they commemorate?

To which of the monuments shown do these facts apply?

It weighs 7000 tonnes.

It was built in 1889.

It is 322 metres (1056 feet) high.

Sir Christopher Wren began work on St Paul's Cathedral in 1688 at the age of 36. He was 78 by the time the great building was finished. Inside is a tablet with a Latin inscription which means *If you seek his monument, look about you.*

TRANSPORT QUIZ

1 What road vehicle gets its name from the town of Kocs in Hungary?

2 In the 1600s, where might you have seen a *turnpike*?
   a) on board ship   b) across a road
   c) on a farm cart

3 In 1769 a remarkable road vehicle made its first journey. Its inventor was a Frenchman called Nicolas Cugnot, and it stopped dead after about 15 minutes. But it was a world first. Can you guess why?

4 Who built the steamship 'Great Eastern', 1858, then the largest ship ever launched?

Did You Know . . .

. . . that W. S. Henson built a model of an 'aerial steam carriage' – in 1843?

. . . that Henri Giffard built a steam-driven airship in 1852?

. . . that a New Zealander known as 'Mad Bird Pearse' may have flown an aeroplane in 1902 – *before* the Wright brothers?

The British Chariot Industry

A famous Roman called Cicero (106–43 BC) once wrote to a friend saying there seemed to be nothing worth bringing away from Britain, except chariots! The Britons had chariots long before the Roman invaders arrived. The British chariot carried two men, a driver and a spear-thrower. It also had a seat, which the Romans had not thought of fitting to their chariots. It was entered from the front and the pole to which the horses were yoked was wide enough for the driver to stand on.

---

5 What kind of machines were the 'R34' and the 'Hindenburg'?

6 In 1927 this pilot made the first solo flight across the Atlantic in the 'Spirit of St Louis'. What was his name?

7 Which famous ocean liner sank after colliding with an iceberg in 1912?

8 The first public railway in the world opened in 1825. Its name?
  a) Liverpool and Manchester
  b) London and Chatham
  c) Stockton and Darlington

9 In September 1783 a sheep, a chicken and a duck made aviation history. How?

10 In what year did the first jet aircraft fly?
  a) 1939   b) 1941   c) 1947

LUCKY DIP

1 Who is the lady with the trident shown on this coin? And what is the link between the date on the coin and Queen Elizabeth II?

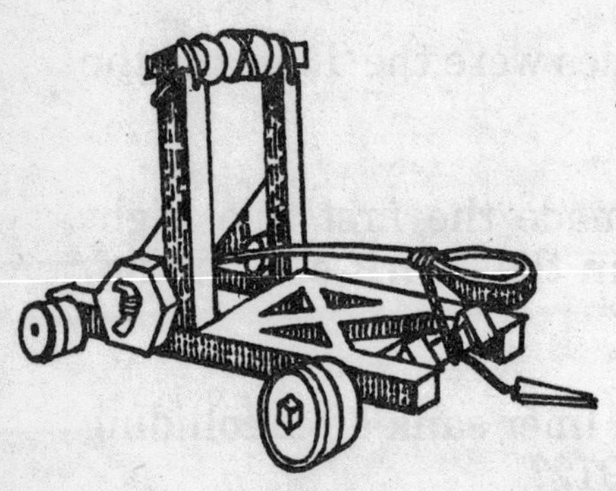

2 Is this strange-looking machine
a) a ducking stool?
b) an irrigation device?
c) a siege weapon for hurling stones?

3 According to legend, in the hills of Greece lived a race of wild creatures, half-human and half-horse. What were they called?

4 In which country did the Opium War and the Boxer Rising take place?

5 What was a *barbican*?
a) a wall protecting a castle gate
b) a medieval war horse
c) A Roman archer

6 This is a picture of one of the Seven Wonders of the Ancient World. Is it
- a) the tomb of Mausolus at Halicarnassus?
- b) the Colossus of Rhodes?
- c) the Pharos of Alexandria?

7 How many countries made up the European Economic Community when it was founded?
a) Six b) Seven c) Nine

8 What was the name of the wall guarding the northern frontier of Roman Britain?

WHERE'S BECHUANALAND?

Sometimes countries change their names. The African state of Botswana, for example, used to be called Bechuanaland.

1 What is the modern name for the country known as the Gold Coast until 1957?

2 In 1981 the republic of Vanuatu became independent. What was its former name?
a) New Malden b) New Hebrides
c) New Guinea

3 Where would you find the Malagasy Republic?
a) Mauritius b) Malaysia c) Madagascar

4 Can you pair up the old and new names of these three African countries?

Malawi	Dahomey
Lesotho	Nyasaland
Benin	Basutoland

5 Marco Polo was the first European traveller to journey to Cathay. What do we call this land today?

Did You Know . . . that Brazil was discovered by mistake? The Portuguese sailor, Cabral, was headed for Africa but steered too far west. He called Brazil the 'Island of the True Cross'.

LOST WORLD

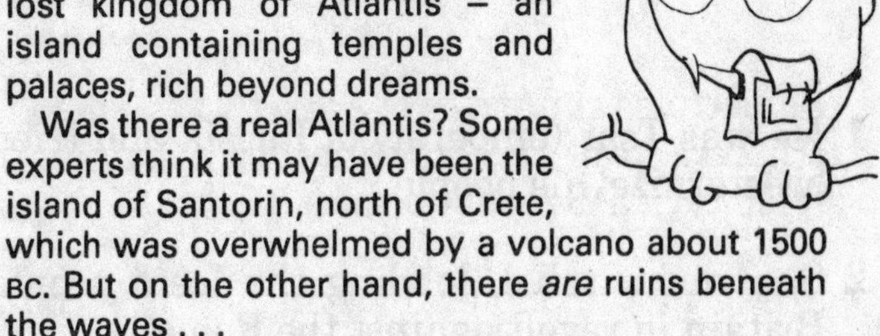

Ancient writers believed in the lost kingdom of Atlantis – an island containing temples and palaces, rich beyond dreams.

Was there a real Atlantis? Some experts think it may have been the island of Santorin, north of Crete, which was overwhelmed by a volcano about 1500 BC. But on the other hand, there *are* ruins beneath the waves . . .

---

6 When first discovered, this island was named Van Diemen's Land. What do we call it now?
a) Tasmania b) Greenland c) Tonga

7 Bosnia, Serbia and Croatia were once all European kingdoms. Of which country are they now part?

8 What was the former name for Iran?
a) Mesopotamia b) Assyria c) Persia

9 What name did East Pakistan take when it broke away from the rest of Pakistan and became independent in 1971?

10 Three countries once made up the Spanish colony of New Granada. Can you work out their modern names, using the spare letters to fill in the gaps?

–O––M––A V–––Z––L– ––U–D–R

O C E A U B E C O E N L E I A

LEADERS

1 He was Tsar (emperor) of Russia and tried to 'westernize' his people.

2 She was a rebel, leading the Iceni people of Britain in revolt against the Romans.

3 This bold sailor led the Vikings across the Atlantic Ocean to land in North America.

4 He was King of the Franks and was crowned Emperor of a new Christian empire in 800 AD.

5 He led the Israelites out of Egypt.

6 A warrior-saint, she led the French to victory against the English.

7 This famous general of Carthage led his army (and elephants) across the Alps.

8 An explorer, who led the first expedition to reach the South Pole in 1911.

9 This soldier-scholar, called the 'father of the English navy', led his people against the Danes.

10 This great conqueror named a town after his horse, Bucephalus.

Clues

ALEXANDER THE GREAT
JOAN OF ARC
ROALD AMUNDSEN
BOADICEA
PETER THE GREAT
HANNIBAL
CHARLEMAGNE
MOSES
ALFRED THE GREAT
LEIF ERICSSON

The Shepherd Boy Who Became King

About 3,000 years ago a shepherd boy lived in Bethlehem. His name was David, and as a child he was named by the prophet Samuel as the next king of Israel.

David became a great fighter. In the battle against the Philistines, he killed the giant Goliath with a stone from his sling.

He was also a skilful musician and played the harp for the old king, Saul. But Saul grew jealous of David's fame and tried to murder him. David had to flee and live for years as an outlaw.

However, after Saul was killed in battle, David did indeed become king of Israel. Unfortunately, he did not always rule wisely and as a result had trouble with his sons, one of whom tried to overthrow him.

HISTORICAL HOWLERS

Can you spot what's wrong with these historical howlers?

1 China clippers were special sailing ships, built to carry porcelain and other fine pottery from the East.

2 King Henry VIII loved food and drink. He grew enormously fat, one reason being the fact that he ate several pounds of potatoes every day.

3 When Cortes landed in Mexico he was amazed to see the wealth of the Aztecs, who greeted him with carts full of gold pulled by white ponies.

4 During the American War of Independence, the colonists and their British rulers met for one last attempt to make peace. This was the so-called 'Boston Tea Party'.

5 The Jacobins were supporters of the Stuart claim to the English throne, and twice rebelled in 1715 and 1745.

6 The 'cat o' nine tails' was a ghostly spectre, reported to have been seen aboard Nelson's flagship 'Victory' the night before Trafalgar.

7 The French king, Louis XIV, owed much to his skilful adviser, Cardinal Marzipan.

8 The *Anglo-Saxon Chronicle* was the first English daily newspaper and was founded by King Alfred the Great.

9 When Spain and England were at war in the 1580s, the King of Spain sent the mighty Armadillo to invade England.

10 The *Communist Manifesto* was the most important work by the 19th-century thinker Groucho Marx.

CHARGE!
(at a gentle trot)

In films (such as *Henry V*) knights on horseback are often shown galloping furiously into battle. In reality armour was so heavy that knights rode large, slow horses.

At the battle of Agincourt, the French knights got jammed together in a narrow open space between trees. They made easy targets for the English archers, and many more French soldiers were trampled by their own clumsy horsemen.

MIDDLE AGES

1 Are the people in the pictures above
a) lords, b) knights, c) villeins,
d) clergy, e) barons?

2 The mounted man (left) in the drawing is Richard I, the Lionheart. He is dressed in the armour of a C-------r.

3 What sort of sport would this bird be used for?

4 This is a familiar figure of the Middle Ages. His clothes were known as 'motley' (at least two colours). He wore tight trousers, close-fitting hood and carried a bauble. Was he . . .

a) master of ceremonies?
b) court jester?
c) major domo?

Chaucer's pilgrims

During the Middle Ages all sorts of people went on journeys to shrines and holy places. They were called pilgrims and the journeys were known as pilgrimages. Often they travelled far from home – to Rome or the Holy Land. In those days the journeys were hazardous, but a pilgrimage was worth the danger, for it was held in high regard by the Church. The most famous pilgrims of the Middle Ages were characters created by the poet Geoffrey Chaucer, whose *Canterbury Tales* are still enjoyed today. Chaucer is shown here as one of the Canterbury pilgrims. He died in 1400.

WHICH CENTURY?

A century is 100 years. When we talk of 'the 18th century', we mean the 1700s – the years between 1700 and 1799. Below are 10 events from history. In which century did each one take place?

1 First underground railway opened.
1700s 1800s 1900s

2 Caxton sets up printing press in London.
1200s 1400s 1600s

3 New Zealand becomes a British colony.
1600s 1700s 1800s

4 Roman army leaves Britain.
400s 500s 600s

5 First King of Belgium chosen.
1200s 1500s 1800s

6 Thirty Years' War is fought in Europe.
1100s 1400s 1600s

7 Jenghiz Khan leads Mongol conquests.
900s 1200s 1400s

8 First Factory Act (to improve working conditions in factories) is passed.
1700s 1800s 1900s

9 Reformation begins in Germany.
1400s 1500s 1600s

10 The Taj Mahal is built.
1400s 1600s 1800s

The Taj Mahal

Built as a tomb for his wife by the Mogul emperor of India, Shah Jahan. Called 'the most beautiful building in the world'. It is made of white marble and 20,000 craftsmen worked on it.

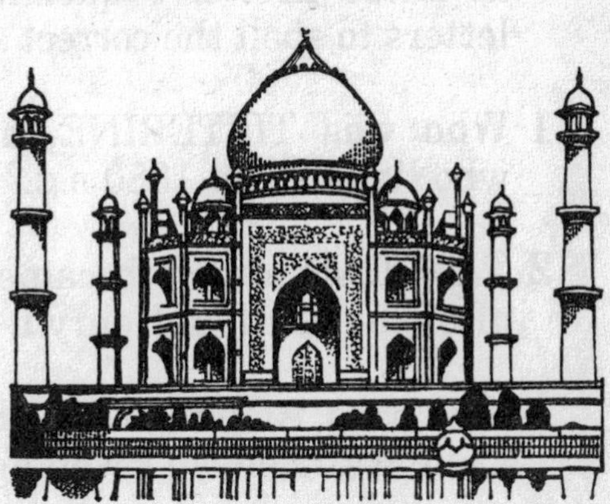

The Hundred Years' War

Did a war really last 100 years? Well, the English and French were at war between 1337 and 1453 (when the French finally won). Occasionally there were great battles, such as Crécy and Agincourt. But there were also long periods when there was hardly any fighting at all. At one point, both sides suffered badly from the great plague known as the Black Death.

What caused the war? Really, the cause went back to William the Conqueror. Ever since 1066 (when William came from France to conquer England) English kings had owned lands in France and often claimed to be kings of France as well as of England. The war began when Edward III of England tried to claim the French throne. It ended with the English having lost all their French lands (except Calais which they kept until 1558).

WOMEN IN HISTORY

In these first five questions, rearrange the letters to spell the correct answer.

1 Who was TIFTERINE, an Egyptian queen who lived about 1380 B.C.?

2 TAMILAD almost became queen of England after the death of Henry I. Who was she?

3 Who was ACABIDOE, who led her tribe of ancient Britons in revolt against the Romans?

4 Who was the French girl, BETTEANDER, who saw a vision of Mary, mother of Jesus, at Lourdes in 1858?

5 Who was LIRACUZE AGROBI, an Italian noble-woman from a powerful and infamous Renaissance family?

6 All these women have been prime ministers of their country. Can you name the country in each case?
a Golda Meir; **b** Gro Harlen Brundtland;
b Indira Gandhi; **d** Margaret Thatcher.

7 What do these four women have in common: Pearl Buck, novelist; Dorothy Hodgkin, chemist; Mother Teresa, nun; and Marie Curie, physicist?

8 Who are these women, who all share the first name *Mary*?

a was executed, on command of her cousin, the queen of England, in 1587.

b was a novelist whose most famous book was called *Frankenstein*.

c was a Scottish missionary who spent many years in Africa.

9 Do you recognize these *Elizabeths*?

a was a prison reformer in England.

b one of the first women doctors, had a London hospital named after her.

c was married to Henry VII of England.

10 Which name would you associate with each of the words in the list below?

a Mary Read
b Rosa Luxemburg
c Sheila Scott
d Vigdis Finnbogadottir
e Mary Kingsley
f Valentina Tereshkova

Explorer
Pirate
Revolutionary
President
Cosmonaut
Aviator

SPORTS QUIZ

1 The modern Olympic Games date from 1896. When were the Games last held in the United Kingdom?

2 Which sport is being described here?
One of the earliest pitches was laid out by Abner Doubleday in 1839. Each team has nine members. The field includes a square known as the 'diamond'.

9 With which sports do you associate a) Arnold Palmer, b) Donald Bradman, c) Joe Louis?

4 The most famous horse race in England was first run in 1780. Its name?

5 The biathlon has been an Olympic sport since 1960. Does this event combine:
a) swimming and horse riding?
b) skiing and rifle shooting?
c) cross country running and archery?

6 What game was Francis Drake playing (so it is said) when news of the Spanish fleet was brought to him in 1588?

7 The North American Indians invented a game they called 'baggataway'. Is its modern name
a) hockey? b) lacrosse? c) basketball?

8 For which sports are these trophies awarded?
a) Davis Cup b) Ryder Cup
c) Calcutta Cup

9 One of the original Olympic events. Modern styles are freestyle (catch-as-catch-can) and Graeco-Roman. Name the sport.

10 When was the first FA Cup Final played?
a) 1865 b) 1872 c) 1901

The First Marathon

Marathon is a place in Greece. In 490 BC a Greek soldier named Pheidippides ran for two days and nights to fetch help against the invading Persians. After running 150 miles, he fought in the Battle of Marathon and raced back to Athens (24 miles) with news of the Greek victory. This last effort was too much, and he fell dead, after gasping out his news. The modern Marathon race is named in his honour.

ROGUES' GALLERY

1 What theft did Colonel Blood attempt in 1671?

2 Edward Teach, Anne Bonny and Henry Morgan were all . . . what?

3 What kind of crime were 'Owlers' and 'Moonrakers' mixed up in?

4 What is the connection between a murderer named Crippen and an early radio set?

5 For what kind of crimes did Tom King and Dick Turpin become notorious?

6 With which country is the outlaw Ned Kelly associated?

HANGING JUDGE

In 1685, after the failure of the Duke of Monmouth's rebellion, King James II of England sent Judge George Jeffreys to deal with the rebels. The furious Judge ordered 320 people to be executed, and about 800 more were sold into slavery in the West Indies.

So many rebels suffered at the hands of the cruel Judge Jeffreys that the trial came to be known as the Bloody Assize. ('Assize' means 'law court'.)

Kidd's Gold

Captain William Kidd (1645–1701) was a privateer. He sailed the Indian Ocean, hunting for French ships and pirates. But he was accused of keeping his prizes for himself, and was hanged at Execution Dock in Wapping, London, where many pirates met a similar fate.

Was Kidd a pirate? Or was he merely trying to carry out his orders from the government? Whatever the truth, people have searched for 'Kidd's Treasure' ever since.

7 Can you complete the names of these three infamous Western desperadoes?

a) Jesse ------ b) ------ the Kid

c) Calamity ----

8 Benedict Arnold, Mata Hari . . . what do these two have in common?

9 With which cities are these criminals associated?

a) Al Capone b) Jack the Ripper

c) Burke and Hare

•Chicago•Rome•New York•Edinburgh•London•

10 'Thugs' were originally gangs of murderers who strangled travellers. To them, murder ('thuggee') was a religious duty. In which country did these thugs live?

KINGS AND QUEENS

1 Fill in the missing 'house' in this list of English kings and queens.

Lancaster
York
Tudor
Stuart
————————
Saxe-Coburg-Gotha

2

Zog	Egypt
Farouk	Swaziland
Victor Emmanuel III	Albania
Sobhuza	Tonga
Taufa' ahau Tupou IV	Italy

The first column lists the names of some 20th-century kings. Only Taufa'ahau Tupou IV still reigns in his country. Can you put the countries on the right in the correct order to pair them with their rulers?

3 Charing Cross is a station in London. The 'cross' was originally one set up by King Edward I of England. It marked the place where his wife's body lay as it was carried from Nottinghamshire to be buried in London. Was Edward's wife . . .

Catherine of Aragon? Margaret of Anjou?
Eleanor of Castile? Caroline of Ansbach?
Philippa of Hainaut?

4 ALouisStrvchaRlesbwcghEnriFpj
Find the names of three French kings in the letters above.

5 Add the first names of these Scottish kings.

K——— MacAlpin D——— Bane
M——— Canmore J——— Balliol
R——— Bruce

6 The Prince Regent became King ——— IV.
Prince Hal became King ——— V.

7 In a pack of playing cards, are the King, Queen and Jack wearing clothes of the reign of a) Henry II b) Henry IV c) Henry VIII?

Kings with No Name

What has the yellow flower called broom to do with a line of English kings?

The Latin name for broom is *Planta genista*, and it seems that Geoffrey, the French Count of Anjou, enjoyed wearing a sprig of broom in his hat. Geoffrey married Matilda, the daughter of Henry I of England, and their son became Henry II. His descendants ruled England until Richard II lost the throne in 1399. During this time the custom grew up of people using surnames, instead of a first name alone. All English families had a surname – except the king's! Richard, Duke of York first used the name 'Plantagenet' in 1448. He was the father of Edward IV. Now all the descendants of Geoffrey of Anjou are called 'Plantagenets' – from the broom he wore in his hat.

WHO DIED . . . ?

1 Who died in these places?

a On the island of St Helena
b In the New Forest while out hunting
c On board HMS 'Victory'
d In an underground bunker in Berlin
e On the way back from the South Pole in 1912

2 According to the stories told about them, who died as a result of . . .

a drinking hemlock while in prison (in ancient Greece)
b being bitten by a poisonous snake called an asp (in ancient Egypt)
c eating too many lampreys (eel-like fishes)
d eating too many peaches
e staying behind in Pompeii after Vesuvius erupted in AD 79

3 An English poet died of a fever while fighting for Greek independence. Who was he?

Wordsworth Keats Byron Shelley

4 A mathematician of ancient Greece died when the Romans attacked the town of Syracuse in Sicily. Who was he?

Pythagoras Archimedes Euclid

Why did Rebels Toast the Little Gentleman in Velvet?

The mole was a hero to the Jacobites, or those Roman Catholics who wanted the Stuarts back as kings of England. They showed how much they admired the little creature by drinking to him, raising their glasses and toasting 'the little gentleman in velvet'. Why?

The Jacobites were supporters of Prince James Edward, 'the Old Pretender' and son of James II, who had been driven into exile in 1688. The new king, William III, was a Protestant. William ruled with his wife, Queen Mary. In 1702 he went out hunting; his horse stumbled over a molehill, and threw the King. As a result of the accident, William died. The Jacobites in exile rejoiced at the news – and drank toasts to the mole! But the Jacobites never won their cause.

REVOLUTION!

The answers to these questions are all to be found among the names in the box at the foot of the page.

1 Who led a group of guerrilla fighters, the 'red shirts', who fought to unite Italy in the mid-19th century?

2 Who was the first Communist leader in the world, following the 1917 Revolution in his country?

3 Who was known as 'The Liberator' because he helped the colonies in South America to become independent from Spain?

4 Who was the German thinker whose political writings inspired many of the Communist revolutions of the 20th century?

LOUIS-NAPOLEON   STALIN   CASTRO

GARIBALDI   ROBESPIERRE   HO CHI MINH

JAMES II   LENIN   SIMON BOLIVAR   CHARLES I

NAPOLEON BONAPARTE   MARX   RICHARD II

PAUL REVERE   MAO TSE-TUNG   GANDHI

5 One of the main figures of the French Revolution, he himself was overthrown and executed in 1784: who was he?

6 Who was king of England at the time that Wat Tyler led the peasants in revolt?

7 This Chinese Communist revolutionary wrote out his thoughts in the 'Little Red Book'. Who was he?

8 Which king of Britain was deposed as a result of the 'Glorious Revolution'?

9 Who was the lawyer who led a revolution in Cuba in 1959?

10 Who became emperor of France after the 1848 revolution?

Picture Question.

On the night before the Americans began their fight for independence from Britain, he rode through the countryside warning people that the war would soon begin. Who was he?

MAKING HISTORY

1 Domesday Book is a list of villages, people, houses, land and animals in England. Which king ordered the list to be made?

Stephen John William I

2 When was the first complete Bible printed in English?

1200 1535 1611

3 Which scientist discovered the Law of Gravitation in 1665?

Pascal Harvey Newton

4 Who tried to found a colony called Virginia in America in 1584? (It failed.)

Raleigh Drake Frobisher

Domesday Book

Domesday Book was drawn up in 1085–86. The king's officials went all over England to find out who owned what. Some parts of the Book are lost, but most of it can still be seen in London. To historians, it is a unique record of life in the middle ages.

5 Who became Kenya's first president in 1964?

Kenyatta Nyerere Banda

6 In what year did British women get the same voting rights as men?

1896 1918 1928

7 Which 'first' took place in the New Mexican desert, USA, on July 16, 1945?

a) the first flight by a jet aircraft
b) the first test of an atomic bomb
c) the first assembly of the UN

8 Which country did Napoleon's Grand Army invade in 1812 – with disastrous results?

Spain Prussia Russia

9 What everyday device was invented by Alexander Graham Bell in 1874?

Telephone Gramophone Light bulb

10 The first airline company to carry passengers by aeroplane started in 1919. Where?

Britain USA France Denmark

ODD ONE OUT

1 One of these was *not* a US President.
Robert E. Lee Herbert Hoover
Harry Truman

2 Who is the odd man out here and why?
Kitchener Jellicoe Haig

3 Which of these battles was not fought at sea?
Sluys Crécy Lepanto Jutland

4 One of these was *not* a Roman emperor.
Augustus Augustine Constantine

5 Which of these countries was *not* a founder member of the EEC or 'Common Market'?
Italy Denmark Luxembourg

6 Spot the explorer who did *not* venture into Darkest Africa.
Mungo Park Daniel Boone Henry Stanley

7 Which of these writers did *not* keep a famous Diary?
Samuel Johnson Samuel Pepys
John Evelyn

8 Who is the odd one out here and why?
Reynolds Constable Chippendale Turner

9 Two of these people were aviation pioneers, the third was more interested in cars.

Daimler Blériot Santos-Dumont

10 Four of these people were alive at the same time, and *could* have met one another. But one just doesn't belong. Can you spot who it is?

Benjamin Franklin Jane Austen
James Watt Florence Nightingale Mozart

DID YOU KNOW?

. . . that William Gilbert, who lived in the time of Queen Elizabeth I, wrote about electricity 300 years before the invention of the electric light bulb?

. . . that a Greek called Hero built a toy that was actually a prototype steam turbine? Hero could not see any practical use for steam power.

. . . that in the Middle Ages a friar called Roger Bacon dreamed of flying machines, and mechanical ships, and discovered how to make gunpowder?

. . . that the first world land speed record (1898) was set not by a petrol-engined vehicle, but by an electric car? Six years later, a steam car reached over 160 km/h (100 mph)!

TWO WORLD WARS

1 Which of these three World War 1 battles was fought at sea?
The Somme Caporetto Jutland

2 Which of these cities did the British General Allenby enter in 1917?
Paris Jerusalem Rome Brussels

3 In what form of fighting did Albert Ball and Manfred von Richthofen become famous?

4 What nickname was given to British troops in World War 1?
Tommies Jerries Doughboys

5 What was the name of the treaty that ended World War 1?
Paris Berlin Versailles

6 Which World War 2 leader declared 'I have nothing to offer but blood, toil, tears and sweat'?

7 What kind of weapon was the German V1 or 'doodlebug'?

8 What happened on a) December 7, 1941; b) June 6, 1944?

9 Was the Battle of Midway (1942) fought on land or at sea, and who took part?

10 Here are three famous faces, belonging to World War 2 leaders. Can you identify them?

At the 11th Hour

The Armistice, or cease-fire, ending the fighting in World War 1 came into effect at 11 a.m. on November 11, 1918 – the eleventh hour of the eleventh day of the eleventh month. After the war, Armistice Day became a special day of remembrance for all who had died in the war.

Mulberries and Pluto

When the Allies invaded France during World War 2, they landed without first capturing a port. Instead they took with them two artificial harbours called 'Mulberries', which were towed across the English Channel. A steel pipe called Pluto (for 'Pipe Line Under the Ocean') was laid on the sea bed to supply oil to the armies.

DIG THIS

These questions are about archaeologists, the people who find and dig up the secrets of the past.

1 Heinrich Schliemann found this object while digging in Asia Minor. It is called the 'Mask of Agamemnon'. But he found no trace of a wooden horse. What city was he searching for?

2 In 1922 Lord Carnarvon and Howard Carter discovered the tomb of an Egyptian pharaoh containing priceless treasures that had been missed by robbers. Who was the pharaoh?

3 Some archaeologists were exploring the ruins of a city. They came across buildings called Temple of Jupiter and Temple of the Vestal Virgins. Which city were they working in?

4 In 1939 archaeologists working in England uncovered the remains of a wooden ship from an ancient mound. The find was at a place called Sutton Hoo. Who built the ship?

a) Anglo-Saxons b) Franks c) Vikings

5 On which island in the Mediterranean is the palace of Knossos? The picture shows a monster which, legend says, lived in a labyrinth on the island. What was it called?

The Roads the Romans Left

Everywhere the Romans went, they built roads. After the Roman Empire collapsed, the fine Roman roads fell into disrepair for people no longer knew how to maintain them. When the Saxons came to Britain and first saw these straight highways of stone, they thought the roads must have been built by gods. People also believed the roads were natural, like trees and rivers. Sometimes they heaped fresh stones on top of the crumbling road in the hope that it would 'grow' a new surface.

Eventually the old Roman roads became so worn and overgrown that they vanished beneath grassland. Old place names mark their passing; for example, 'Streatham' – from the old Saxon word for 'street'. Aerial photos can now trace long-hidden roads criss-crossing the countryside, unseen by people on the ground. Long-lost farms, villas and forts are also revealed by the camera as shadowy outlines.

TRUE OR FALSE?

Some of these statements are true. Some are false. All you have to do is choose!

1 Shinto was an ancient game, rather like hockey, played by the Scottish Highlanders.

2 The Romans ate ice cream.

3 A toreador was a wandering minstrel during the Middle Ages.

4 King Charles I went to the scaffold wearing two shirts so he would not shiver and cause people to believe he was afraid to die.

5 The religions of Judaism, Christianity and Islam all arose in the Middle East, and Judaism is the oldest.

6 Louis XIV of France was called the 'Sun King' because he once danced the part of the Sun in a court ballet.

7 Rome has been Italy's capital since 1480.

8 The first explorer to reach the North Pole was the Norwegian, Amundsen, in 1909.

9 Adolf Hitler, the German dictator, was born in Austria.

10 The source of the River Nile was discovered by David Livingstone in 1871.

11 The first ice skates were made from cow ribs and similar bones.

12 The first (and for a long time only) transport animal used by North American Indians was the dog.

STRANGE . . . BUT TRUE

The capital of Iceland is Reykjavik. It was founded in 874 by a group of Norsemen. As they sailed inshore, their leader, Ingolfur Arnarson, threw into the sea two timbers from his old house in Norway and vowed he would build his new home at the spot where the wood drifted ashore. They were found near some hot, steaming springs, so the place was named Reykjavik or 'smoky bay'.

In the 1700s rich women's hairstyles were very elaborate, made stiff with grease or even built up on a wire frame. On top were mounted flowers, model ships and even miniature battles with toy soldiers! Because mice were attracted to sleepers by the wheat or rice meal powder used to dress the hair, 'mouse-proof wire night caps' were offered for sale.

HISTORY TODAY

This quiz is all about events and people in the news during the last 20 years.

1 Which East European country was invaded by the USSR in 1968?
East Germany   Poland   Czechoslovakia

2 Who was US President after John F. Kennedy (assassinated in 1963)?
Lyndon Johnson   Richard Nixon
Jimmy Carter

3 In 1979 the Shah was overthrown. What country did the Shah rule?

4 In 1976 two unmanned spacecraft landed on the planet Mars. What were they called?
Pioneer   Viking   Voyager

5 What is the nationality of the present Pope, John Paul II?

6 Who celebrated her silver jubilee in 1977? And what did her 'silver jubilee' mark?

7 A Russian broke every previous human speed record in 1961. What did he do?

8 Who was *third* in succession to the throne of the United Kingdom on January 1, 1983?

9 In 1967 Dr Christiaan Barnard made medical history with a surgical 'first'. What did he do?

10 With which countries do you associate these leaders?

MITTERRAND	WEST GERMANY
ANDROPOV	INDIA
KOHL	AUSTRALIA
TRUDEAU	USSR
GANDHI	CANADA
HAWKE	FRANCE

WHAT YEAR?

In which year did the following events take place?

Ronald Reagan was sworn in as US President

Space shuttle 'Columbia' made its first flight in orbit

The Prince of Wales and Lady Diana Spencer were married

In tennis, McEnroe beat Borg in the men's singles at Wimbledon

Antigua and Barbuda (in the West Indies) became independent

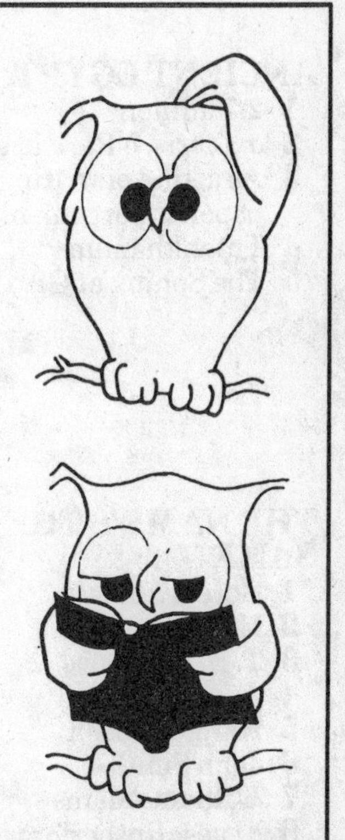

ANSWERS

STONE AGE QUIZ

1 *a*
2 how to hunt (farming did not begin until about 10,000 years ago)
3 A bison (this drawing is based on one in the Altamira Cave in Spain)

ANCIENT EGYPT

1 2.3 million
2 *a* Osiris, *b* Ra, *c* Isis
3 As a kind of writing paper or parchment
4 Tutankhamun
5 The Sphinx at Giza

THE NAME'S THE SAME

1 Gerald Ford
2 Mary Kingsley
3 T. E. Lawrence
4 Amy Johnson
5 Harold Wilson
6 John Smith
7 William Adams
8 Ernest Rutherford

FAMOUS SHIPS

1 'Mayflower'
2 'Beagle'
3 *b*
4 'Victory'
5 John Paul Jones
6 'Graf Spee'
7 'United States'
8 'Mary Rose'
9 *a*
10 'Revenge' = Grenville
'Golden Hind' = Drake
'Endeavour' = Cook
'Santa Maria' = Columbus

WILD WEST

1 Wyatt Earp (1848–1929)
2 *a* Billy the Kid, *b* Buffalo Bill, *c* Calamity Jane
3 A covered waggon
4 The joining of the two railroads spanning the USA, the Union Pacific (building west) and the Central Pacific (building east)
5 A lasso
6 General George Custer, leading the US 7th Cavalry
7 Leather or hide coveralls to protect a cowboy's legs from thorns
8 Apache
9 Davy Crockett

FACT OR FICTION?

1 Fiction (No real proof of a real-life Robin Hood exists, although there are several 'possibles')
2 Fact
3 Fact
4 Fact
5 Fiction (Tales of King Arthur and his Knights are based on a number of very old stories)
6 Fact
7 Fact
8 Fact
9 Fact
10 Fiction (created by Sir Arthur Conan Doyle)
11 Fact
12 Fiction (created by Baroness Orczy)

WHEN IN ROME

1 Romulus and Remus
2 River Tiber
3 *b*
4 Latin
5 Geese
6 *a* False
b True
c False (Jupiter was king of the Roman gods)
7 Plebeians
8 Colosseum

Picture Question.
Patrician; Toga; Senator; Purple

FAMOUS BATTLES

Picture Puzzle.
1 = Concentration, 2 = Co-operation, 3 = Luck, 4 = Surprise, 5 = Mobility

1 Marathon
2 Agincourt
3 Tshushima
4 Hastings
5 Yorktown
6 Alamein

REFORMERS

1 Abraham Lincoln
2 *a* Eros (the Greek god of love)
b Shaftesbury
3 A council called to question Martin Luther
4 Florence Nightingale
5 Helping to abolish slavery
6 *a* William Penn
b Philadelphia
7 VOTES FOR WOMEN
Emmeline Pankhurst

EUREKA!

1 Copernicus
2 Bacon wanted to know if the snow would stop the meat from going bad–an early attempt at deep-freezing food!
3 Priestley = oxygen
Fleming = penicillin
Jenner = vaccination
4 1000
5 Newton = gravity;
Einstein = relativity;
Trevithick = steam locomotive;
Lister = antiseptics;
Pascal = calculating machine;
Marconi = radio telegraphy;
Roentgen = X-rays
6 Lightning conductor rod

PRIME MINISTERS

1 Charles James Fox
2 Duke of Wellington
3 Pitt the Younger
4 Disraeli
5 Harold Wilson (aged 48 in 1964)
6 Ramsay MacDonald
7 Gladstone
8 1979
9 Robert Peel
10 Chamberlain
11 Sri Lanka (Mrs Bandaranaike, 1960)
12 De Valera = Ireland;
Menzies = Australia;
Pearson = Canada;
Pompidou = France;
Holyoake = New Zealand

WHO WAS . . . ?

1 Wat Tyler
2 P. T. Barnum
3 Sigmund Freud
4 Marie Curie
5 Ulysses S. Grant
6 Marie Antoinette
7 Brigham Young
8 James Wolfe
9 Abel Tasman
10 Otto von Bismarck
11 Amelia Earhart
12 Edward Jenner

Mystery Man. Charles Stuart, the Young Pretender, known as 'Bonny Prince Charlie'

INITIALS QUIZ

1 Union of Soviet Socialist Republics
2 United Nations
3 European Economic Community
4 Organization of African Unity
5 Federal Bureau of Investigation
6 North Atlantic Treaty Organization
7 Great Britain
8 World Health Organization
9 Southeast Asia Treaty Organization
10 Strategic Arms Limitation Treaty
11 United Nations International Children's Emergency Fund
12 United Kingdom
13 United Nations Educational, Scientific and Cultural Organization

WARRIORS

1 Achilles (who as a baby was dipped into the River Styx by his mother, only his heel being untouched by its magical waters)
2 *b*
3 The Roman army; a centurion was a non-commissioned officer, a cohort was a unit of from 400 to 600 men
4 *a* = Greek, *b* = 13th century, *c* = Norman, *d* = Roman
5 Japan

WHAT DID THEY WEAR?

1 Toga
2 Doublet
3 Crinoline
4 Knickerbockers
5 Kirtle

Picture Puzzle. *a* Ancient Egyptian, *b* early 1200s, *c* Puritans 1640, *d* about 1905, *e* 1800 to 1820, *f* about 1840, *g* 1920s, *h* Ancient Greek

PRESIDENTIAL PUZZLERS

1 Washington
2 Jefferson
3 Lincoln
4 Nixon
5 Wilson
6 Truman
7 Eisenhower
8 Kennedy
9 Carter

Puzzle. Harding; Adams; Taft; Reagan; Nixon; Grant; Hoover

WHO SAID . . . ?

1 *Let them eat cake*
2 Henry Ford
3 *Veni Vidi Vici*
4 Richard III
5 A = Napoleon
B = Charles II
C = H. M. Stanley
D = Louis XIV
E = Henry II
F = Abraham Lincoln
G = Edith Cavell
6 Queen Victoria
7 George Washington

FAMOUS DATES

1 To escape the Great Fire of London
2 He was at the Battle of Waterloo. Copenhagen was the Duke of Wellington's horse. Waterloo is near Brussels
3 The Roman invasion of Britain. Ancient Britons painted themselves with woad, which was blue
4 Christopher Columbus, in the *Pinta, Niña* and *Santa Maria*
5 Gold was discovered, and the 'gold rush' followed
6 The Spanish Armada was sighted
7 William the Conqueror defeated the English at the Battle of Hastings. The event is shown on the Bayeux Tapestry
8 It was for the first public passenger train in the world, George Stephenson's *Locomotion No. 1*
9 The USSR, following the Russian Revolution
10 The potato crop had failed and there was a famine
11 On the Moon

ASSASSINATIONS

1 Gandhi
2 Borgias
3 Richard III
4 Julius Caesar
5 *a* Theatre; Dallas
b US Presidents
6 Mary Queen of Scots
7 World War 1
8 Trotsky

MONUMENTS

1 The Monument in the City of London, marking the starting point of the Great Fire of 1666
2 The Arc de Triomphe in Paris, set up to celebrate Napoleon's victories
3 Nelson's Column in Trafalgar Square, London: monument to Admiral Lord Nelson
4 Statue of Liberty, New York, USA; a gift from the French people in 1886, 100 years after the Declaration of Independence
5 Mount Rushmore, S. Dakota, USA bears carved heads of Washington, Jefferson, Lincoln and Theodore Roosevelt
6 The Eiffel Tower, built for the Paris Exhibition, 100 years after the French Revolution
The 'vital statistics' are those of the Eiffel Tower

TRANSPORT QUIZ

1. The coach
2. *b*, a turnpike was a barrier; travellers had to pay a toll to pass it
3. It was the world's first steam-driven vehicle, the first automobile
4. Isambard Kingdom Brunel
5. Airships
6. Charles Lindbergh
7. 'Titanic'
8. *c*
9. They ascended in a Montgolfier balloon, the first living creatures to do so
10. *a* (the German He 178)

LUCKY DIP

1. Britannia; 1953 was the date of the Queen's coronation
2. *c*, it was called a trebuchet
3. Centaurs
4. China
5. *a*
6. *c*, it was a lighthouse, built about 280 BC. It collapsed in an earthquake in 1375
7. *a*
8. Hadrian's Wall

WHERE'S BECHUANALAND?

1. Ghana
2. *b*
3. *c*
4. Malawi was Nyasaland
   Lesotho was Basutoland
   Benin was Dahomey
5. China
6. *a*
7. Yugoslavia
8. *c*
9. Bangladesh
10. Colombia, Venezuela, Ecuador

LEADERS

1 Peter the Great
2 Boadicea
3 Leif Ericsson
4 Charlemagne
5 Moses
6 Joan of Arc
7 Hannibal
8 Roald Amundsen
9 Alfred the Great
10 Alexander the Great

HISTORICAL HOWLERS

1 China clippers in fact brought tea from China
2 Henry never ate potatoes; they were unknown in England until Sir Walter Raleigh introduced them from America
3 The Aztecs had neither horses, nor carts. (Cortes and his Spaniards brought horses with them)
4 The Boston Tea Party happened before the war, in 1773. Angry colonists tipped tea into Boston Harbour as a protest against paying British taxes
5 It was the *Jacobites* who supported the Stuart cause. *Jacobins* were revolutionaries during the French Revolution, 1793–4 period
6 The 'cat' was not a ghost, but it was feared–it was a whip used to punish wrongdoers
7 The Cardinal's real name was MAZARIN
8 The *Chronicle* was a history of England, not a newspaper
9 The Spaniards sailed in the ARMADA, not an ARMADILLO (which is a South American animal)
10 KARL Marx, not GROUCHO (a famous film comedian)

MIDDLE AGES

1 *a* Villeins (peasants)
2 Crusader
3 Hawking or Falconry
4 *b* Court jester

WHICH CENTURY?

1 1800s (1890)
2 1400s (1476)
3 1800s (1840)
4 400s (407)
5 1800s (1831)
6 1600s (1618–48)
7 1200s (1206–27)
8 1800s (1833)
9 1500s (1517)
10 1600s (1632–50)

WOMEN IN HISTORY

1 Nefertiti
2 Matilda
3 Boadicea
4 Bernadette
5 Lucrezia Borgia
6 *a* Israel; *b* Norway
c India; *d* U.K.
7 They all won Nobel prizes
8 *a* Mary, Queen of Scots
b Mary Shelley
c Mary Slessor
9 *a* Elizabeth Fry
b Elizabeth Garrett Anderson
c Elizabeth of York
10 *a* Pirate
b Revolutionary
c Aviator
d President
e Explorer
f Cosmonaut

SPORTS QUIZ

1 1948, London
2 Baseball
3 *a* golf, *b* cricket, *c* boxing
4 The Derby
5 *b*
6 Bowls
7 *b*
8 *a* tennis, *b* golf,
c rugby football
9 Wrestling
10 *b*

ROGUES' GALLERY

1 He tried (unsuccessfully) to steal the Crown Jewels
2 Pirates (or buccaneers)
3 Smuggling
4 A radio message to the ship on which the murderer was escaping to the USA led to his capture. This was in 1909, and was probably the first time radio was used to track and catch a criminal
5 They were English highwaymen
6 Australia
7 *a* Jesse James
b Billy the Kid
c Calamity Jane
8 They were both spies
9 *a* Chicago
b London
c Edinburgh
10 India

KINGS AND QUEENS

1 Hanover
2 Zog = Albania; Farouk = Egypt; Victor Emmanuel III = Italy; Sobhuza = Swaziland; Taufa'ahau Tupou IV = Tonga
3 Eleanor of Castile
4 Louis, Charles, Henri
5 Kenneth MacAlpin; Malcolm Canmore; Donald Bane; John Balliol; Robert Bruce
6 George; Henry
7 Henry VIII

WHO DIED?

1 *a* Napoleon
b William Rufus
c Nelson
d Hitler
e Scott
2 *a* Socrates
b Cleopatra
c King Henry I
d King John
e Pliny the Elder
3 Byron
4 Archimedes

REVOLUTION!

1 Giuseppe Garibaldi
2 Lenin
3 Simon Bolivar
4 Karl Marx
5 Maximilien Robespierre
6 Richard II
7 Mao Tse-tung
8 James II
9 Fidel Castro
10 Louis-Napoleon

Picture Question.
Paul Revere

MAKING HISTORY

1 William I
2 1535
3 Newton
4 Raleigh
5 Kenyatta
6 1928
7 *b*
8 Russia
9 Telephone
10 Denmark

ODD ONE OUT

1 Robert E. Lee
2 Jellicoe (an admiral, the others were generals)
3 Crécy
4 Augustine
5 Denmark
6 Daniel Boone
7 Johnson
8 Chippendale, who was a furniture-maker
9 Daimler
10 Florence Nightingale (she was born in 1820, by which time all the others were dead)

TWO WORLD WARS

1 Jutland
2 Jerusalem
3 In the air; they were fighter 'aces'
4 Tommies
5 Versailles (signed 1919)
6 Winston Churchill
7 A flying bomb, with a jet engine
8 *a* Pearl Harbor, when Japan attacked the USA
b D-Day, the start of the Allied invasion of occupied France
9 At sea, between the US and Japanese Pacific fleets
10 *a* Joseph Stalin
b Adolf Hitler
c Franklin D. Roosevelt

DIG THIS

1 Troy
2 Tutankhamun
3 Rome
4 Anglo-Saxons
5 Crete; The Monster, half man and half bull, was called the Minotaur

TRUE OR FALSE?

1 False: *Shinto* is the Japanese form of Buddhism; the Highland game is *shinty*
2 True: they ate fruit mixed with snow
3 False: a *toreador* is a Spanish bullfighter (although the word is not used nowadays). Wandering minstrels were *troubadors*
4 True
5 True
6 True
7 False: Italy was not united until 1861. Rome did not become Italy's capital until 1871
8 False: it was the American, Peary
9 True
10 False: it was discovered by John Hanning Speke in 1862
11 True
12 True (horses had died out before the time of the modern Indians, and were reintroduced by the Spanish)

HISTORY TODAY

1 Czechoslovakia
2 Lyndon Johnson
3 Iran
4 Viking
5 Polish
6 Queen Elizabeth II, marking 25 years of her reign (1952–77)
7 Yuri Gagarin became the first man to orbit the Earth in space
8 Prince Andrew, after Prince Charles and Prince William (born 1982)
9 He carried out the first heart transplant operation
10 Mitterrand = France; Andropov = USSR; Kohl = West Germany; Trudeau = Canada; Gandhi = India; Hawke = Australia

What Year? Answer: 1981

How did you do?
Better than you expected?
Worse?
You never liked history anyway?
Too frightened even to
look at the answers?

If you scored about 50% – that's 5 out of 10 on the 10-question quizzes – we reckon you did pretty well.

If you got *every* question right, in any one of the quizzes, well done!

And if you didn't score very well, don't worry. You'll almost certainly do better next time! Especially if you do a little 'research' to boost your performance as a quiz star.
So don't forget Children's Britannica – the encyclopaedia with all the answers!